About the Book

Lightning crackled across the darkening sky. The wind whistled through the trees and swept up high waves all around. Then suddenly the rain came pouring down, soaking little Wood Duck Baby as he paddled along the pond. He could see his family swimming farther and farther away as he tried to catch up with them. Soon he would be lost and all alone! What could he do?

Wood Duck Baby's adventures growing up in the wild will fascinate young children in this easy-to-read book about the everyday life of a little duckling. From his springtime birth till he is fully grown in autumn, Wood Duck Baby's spunky resourcefulness will help him survive nature's hardships.

WOOD DUCK BABY

by Berniece Freschet
pictures by Jim Arnosky

A See & Read Book

G.P. Putnam's Sons · New York

For Adam Young, with special love

Text copyright © 1983 by Berniece Freschet.
Illustrations copyright © 1983 by Jim Arnosky.
All rights reserved. Published simultaneously in Canada
by General Publishing Co. Limited, Toronto.
Printed in the United States of America.
Library of Congress Cataloging in Publication Data
Freschet, Berniece.
Wood duck baby.
(A See & Read book)
Summary: Describes the development and day-to-day
activities of a wood duck from birth to mating.
1. Wood-duck—Juvenile literature.
2. Animals, Infancy of—Juvenile literature. [1. Ducks]
I. Arnosky, Jim, ill. II. Title III. Series.
QL696.A52F73 1983 598.4'1 82-13250
ISBN 0-399-61191-6
First impression.

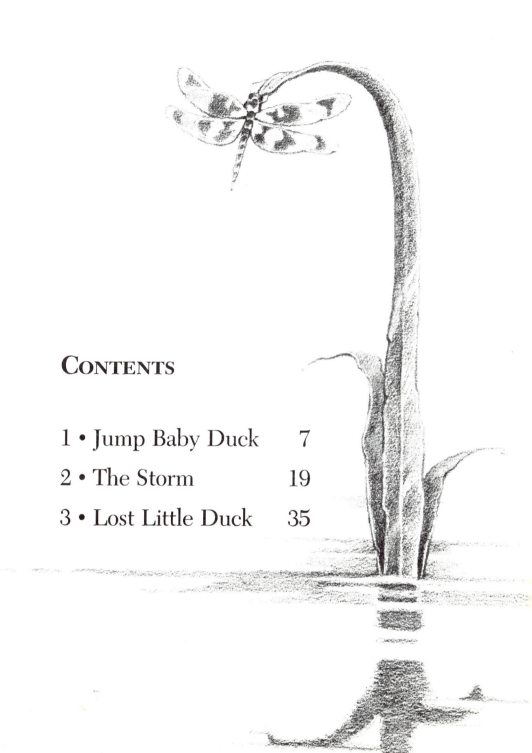

Contents

1 • Jump Baby Duck

The wood duck flew

through the woods.

Up and down she flew.

Over and under the tree limbs.

At the edge of the woods,

she sat on a limb

and looked all around.

But no enemy was near.

Quickly she popped into a hole.

Inside the tree she sat down

on her nest of eggs.

It was March.

Every day, for the last twelve days,

the wood duck had laid an egg.

Now it was time to brood the eggs—

to sit on them and keep them warm.

Most ducks hide their nests

in grasses on the ground.

But the wood duck makes her
nest in a hollow tree or stump.
She feels safer there.
The wood duck only left her nest to eat.

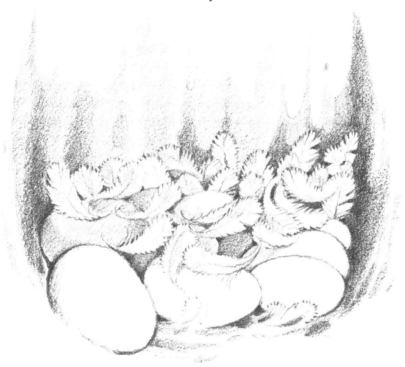

Before she left, she covered her eggs
with down that she had plucked
from her breast.
The soft feathers kept her eggs warm.

One late afternoon, when she was away,

a hungry raccoon climbed the tree.

He was looking for a supper of eggs.

He pushed his nose into the hole.

He smelled wood duck.

He tried to get inside but the hen

had picked a hole too small

for the raccoon to get into.

She knew enemies would eat her eggs.

The raccoon did not give up.

He pushed his paw down into the tree.

His long fingers closed over an egg.

He pulled it up and ate it.

He reached down for another.

He would eat them all if he could.

But he could reach only one more.

The rest of the eggs were safe.

For thirty days

the wood duck sat on her nest,

leaving only to eat.

On the thirty-first day

there was a sound of tapping.

A baby duck tapped on the shell

with the sharp tooth on its bill.

Tap—tap—tap.

Wood duck baby wanted to get out.

The tapping went on

all day and all night.

The next day the egg had a crack.

Suddenly, the eggshell broke open.

A tiny wet head poked out.

Wood duck baby lay in the nest.

Before long, nine other baby ducks

broke out of their shells.

Peep—peep—peep,

called the little baby ducks.

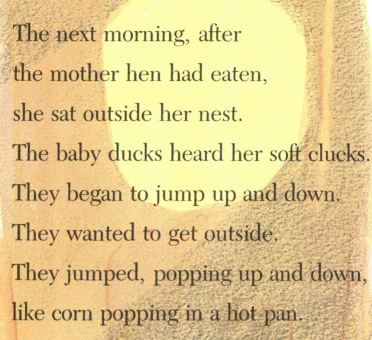

The next morning, after
the mother hen had eaten,
she sat outside her nest.
The baby ducks heard her soft clucks.
They began to jump up and down.
They wanted to get outside.
They jumped, popping up and down,
like corn popping in a hot pan.

The baby ducks had sharp claws
on the tips of their webbed feet.
The claws stuck into the tree.
Jump by jump, wood duck baby
hopped up to the hole and looked out.
Inside, the nest was dark and cozy.
But outside the world was big and bright.
His mother called to him.

It was a long way down.

But he was not afraid.

Wood duck baby stretched out

his fuzzy little wings and jumped.

Down he fell, rolling and tumbling

over the soft grass.

Wood duck baby was not hurt.

One by one, all the little ducks

tumbled down to the ground.

The mother hen led them to the pond.

In a long line,

the ducklings ran after her

and wood duck baby was first in line.

2 • THE STORM

It was April.

The beaver pond was full of life.

The air was filled with

the sounds of spring—

birds singing, insects buzzing

and the croaking of frogs.

There were other ducks at the pond.

Teal, pintail and mallard ducks

swam with their young.

A family of Canada geese and

two white swans swam with their babies.

Each family stayed together.

The little wood ducks paddled

after their mother across the pond.

They came to a patch of green pond weeds

and stopped to feed.

Close by, two male wood ducks
were also feeding.
One was the hen's mate.
He had flown with her when
she looked for the nesting tree.
But she saw little of him
after she began to brood her eggs.

21

The hen's feathers were
mostly grey and brown.
But the male drake's
feathers were greens, and purples
and blues that gleamed in the sun.
Two white lines of feathers
went from his bill to the tip
of the crest on his head.

His neck and throat were white.

He had red eyes, and a red and white bill.

Bold lines and spots
of black and white feathers
marked his sides.

The wood duck family swam on.
They passed the beaver's house
of mud and sticks.

A mother beaver sat on top
with her three new kits.
A water snake swam close.

The mother hen spread her wings
and hissed loudly.

If he was hungry the snake
might grab one of the ducklings.
But the snake had just had a meal
of tadpoles, and all he wanted
was a warm place to nap.

The mother hen and her ducklings
paddled on, stopping often
to nibble on the water weeds.
Late in the day the mother hen
led her tired family up the bank
and under a bush to rest.
Wood duck baby snuggled close
to his mother and was soon asleep.
The family did not go back
to their nest in the tree.
Now they slept under shrubs and bushes.

It was a dangerous time
for the little ducks.
They could swim but they could not yet fly.
The mother hen kept
a careful watch for enemies:
the big bass, the snapping turtle,
the muskrat, the otter,
the water snake and the weasel.

The mother hen watched over
her babies as best she could.
But one day the snapping turtle
pulled a duckling under the water!
And then another little duck was
snatched up in the talons of a hawk!
Now only eight ducklings
swam beside their mother.

One day the sky grew dark.

Lightning flashed.

The wind blew.

Thunder crashed.

As waves of water splashed high,

the little ducks bobbed up and down.

Mother hen hurried her babies to the shore.

Wood duck baby paddled hard.
But the wind pushed him back.
He tried to stay with the others
but a wave pulled at him.
He called to his mother.
But she could not hear his call
over the howling of the wind.

Wood duck baby struggled.

It was no use.

The wind and waves carried

him farther and farther away.

Wood duck baby was lost—and alone.

3 • LOST LITTLE DUCK

Wood duck baby needed
a safe place to rest.
The wind blew him under a bush.
He pushed up into the willows,
where he spent the long night,
huddled in a small round ball.
The next morning the sun shone bright
in the blue sky.
Wood duck baby ate some seeds
and felt stronger.

He looked for his family.

He must find his mother soon,

before an enemy found him.

Peep—peep, he called.

He heard a splash close by.

He scurried into the reeds to hide.

It was only a green frog.

Wood duck baby swam on his way.

Far off, he heard a duck call.

Was it his family?

Wood duck baby paddled faster.

Then around the reeds
came a family of swans.
They swam past,
away from the lost little duck.

Wood duck baby
came to the beaver house.
He saw a ripple on the water.
It came close—and closer.

An old water snake lifted his head.
He was hungry and looking for food.
Wood duck baby was very still.
Today the little duck was lucky.

The water snake did not see him
and swam away.
Wood duck baby hopped onto
the beaver house.

Then, suddenly, around the side of the

beaver house swam the wood ducks.

Wood duck baby jerked his head high.

PEEP—PEEP! he called.

When mother hen swam close and called,

the lost little duck

jumped into the water.

Wood duck baby was safe at last.

All his brothers and sisters

peeped loudly,

as if happy to see their brother again.

Now only seven little ducklings

swam beside their mother.

One other had been lost in the storm.

Every day the ducklings grew bigger.
The mother hen began to molt.
She grew new feathers in place of
the worn and broken old ones.

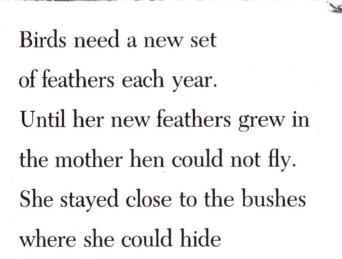

Birds need a new set
of feathers each year.
Until her new feathers grew in
the mother hen could not fly.
She stayed close to the bushes
where she could hide
if an enemy came near.

As the little ducks grew
they spent more time on land
eating seeds and acorns.
At night they roosted in the trees.
When the mother hen's new feathers
had finished growing,
she took her family to join
other groups of wood ducks.

It was autumn.

Red and yellow leaves

floated in circles on the water.

Wood duck baby was fully grown

and very handsome.

His feathers had the bright

colors of the male drake.

As the nights grew cool,

more and more water birds came.

Soon the flocks
would fly south for the winter.
But in the spring,
wood duck would return,
bringing his new mate
to the beaver pond.

The birds would be singing,
the insects buzzing
and hundreds of frogs croaking.

Together, wood duck and his mate
would look for their own nest.
A safe hidden place
deep in a hollow tree.

And in the spring, wood duck's babies
would jump from their nest
to swim in the beaver pond.